PowerKiDS
Readers
SEA FRIENDS

HARP SEALS

SAM DRUMLIN

PowerKiDS
press™

New York

Published in 2013 by The Rosen Publishing Group, Inc.
29 East 21st Street, New York, NY 10010

First Edition

Editor: Amelie von Zumbusch
Book Design: Liz Gloor and Colleen Bialecki

Photo Credits: Cover John Giustina/Taxi/Getty Images; p. 5 Florida Stock/Shutterstock.com; p. 7 Hiroyuki Matsumoto/Photographer's Choice/Getty Images; p. 9 iStockphoto.com/Thinkstock; p. 11 Vladimir Melnik/Shutterstock.com; p. 13 Ralph Lee Hopkins/National Geographic/Getty Images; pp. 15, 23 Jupiter Images/Photos.com/Thinkstock; p. 17 © Minden Pictures/Superstock; p. 19 AleksandrN/Shutterstock.com; p. 21 Tom Brakefield/Stockbyte/Thinkstock.

Library of Congress Cataloging-in-Publication Data

Drumlin, Sam.
  Harp seals / by Sam Drumlin. — 1st ed.
    p. cm. — (Powerkids readers: sea friends)
  Includes index.
  ISBN 978-1-4488-9646-2 (library binding) — ISBN 978-1-4488-9750-6 (pbk.) —
  ISBN 978-1-4488-9751-3 (6-pack)
  1. Harp seal—Juvenile literature. I. Title.
  QL737.P64D78 2013
  599.79'29—dc23
                            2012024548

Manufactured in the United States of America

CPSIA Compliance Information: Batch #W13PK3: For Further Information contact Rosen Publishing, New York, New York at 1-800-237-9932

CONTENTS

Harp seals are cute!

They live in the sea.

Babies are **pups**.

They are soft.

They are born on **ice floes**.

Pups nurse for about two weeks.

In time, pups grow new **coats**.

They learn to swim.

Fish are their main food.

They grow new coats
each year.

WORDS TO KNOW

coat

ice floes

pup

INDEX

WEBSITES

Due to the changing nature of Internet links, PowerKids Press has developed an online list of websites related to the subject of this book. This site is updated regularly. Please use this link to access the list: www.powerkidslinks.com/pkrsf/hseal/